D1331936

Are you ready?

JOHN CORLESS

salmonpoetry

Published in 2009 by
Salmon Poetry
Cliffs of Moher, County Clare, Ireland
Website: www.salmonpoetry.com
Email: info@salmonpoetry.com

Copyright © John Corless 2009

ISBN 978-1-907056-16-1

Cover artwork: *Leaves with water drops* by Vasiliy Koval, from dreamstime.com
Cover design & typesetting: Siobhán Hutson
Printed in England by imprint*digital*.net

To the people who refuse to lie under the juggernaut of depression sweeping Ireland. To the rest: read on and cheer up.

Acknowledgements

Acknowledgements are due to the following in which some of these poems were previously published or broadcast:

Mid West Radio; Liveline, RTE Radio One; Playback, RTE Radio One; Machias Valley News Observer; and Markings.

Contents

Are you ready?   11

Daily Worship   12

Dear Father John Paul,   14

Single woman, 38, broadminded, gsoh, considered
good looking, wanting more from life, breaks it off
with bachelor farmer, 56   17

Days of Fake Tan   19

A Romantic Irishman's Gift to His Wife
on Valentine's Day   23

Anything to Declare?   24

Date As Postmark   27

Misé Eire 2009   28

Testing   29

House to Yourself   31

Hooded Crows   32

Ritual   33

Paddy Naughton   37

Abandoned Railway   40

Never Black   43

Your Field   44

Posts and Wire   45

They Cut-down the Trees   46

Mick Donlon   49

The Waking   50

A Life   51

Lovers   52

Going Through Your Things   53

Ireland – October 4th, 2005   54

Removal   55

A Different Way of Life   57

Vision   59

Nothing   60

Autumn 1944   61

By the Fire   63

Object of Desire   64

Dad   65

Shrine   66

Kidney and Clutch Kebabs   67

And Another Thing   68

And On Sundays   69

18   70

In Farmers Fields   72

Election Manifesto   73

Visitors   75

The Journey   76

An Open Letter to the Purchasing Department of
Mid West Farmers Co-Operative Society; All other
Farmers Co-Operative Societies Please Copy   78

Disgusting   82

Oh To Own My Own Chip Shop   84

Half-Eleven Mass   87

Are you ready?

When the row with the wife has gone
on for over a week and your neck
and lower back hurt from sleeping
on the dirty green sofa –
and when the chips you got in McDonalds
Drive-Thru fall in to the space
around the handbrake and you're sorry
now that your toe-nail clippings
are still there, and you made the mistake
of putting your only white shirt
into the washing machine
along with the lawnmower,
are you ready?

Are you ready to admit that it was you
who ran over Bozo in 1997 and broke
his front legs, that the hundred pounds
she saved for Santa went on the fourth
placed certainty in the three-ten at Newmarket,
that it was you who ran up the phone bill
on the sex lines,
that you do sometimes drink and drive,
that you occasionally wear
your wife's lingerie,
that the job interview really was golf,
that you do secretly fancy Susan Kelly,
that you once voted for the PDs?

Are you ready?
Are you ready to admit?
Are you ready to admit
that maybe it was you that was in the wrong
all along?

Daily Worship

Delighted that Father Loula, the Parish Priest
has contracted a small bout of Alzheimers,
Father John Paul is pleased to have gotten
the weekday morning Mass gig.

Today, he moves his chair slightly to the left
as Mrs. Dolan, a woman he can't stand,
obscures his view of Olivia –
the national school teacher and daily Communicant

seated in the fourth row.
He watches as she attentively listens
as Sr. Cuntata reads from the letters
to the Hebrews, and wishes that the Psalm

of his right hand was on her left knee,
Olivia's, not Sr. Cuntata's –
whose knee last saw the light of day
on the 9th. May 1942.

Father John Paul, for whom his mother,
sitting in the front row, has hopes
he will one day ascend to the highest calling –
like his famous namesake,

can't wait for Holy Communion,
his favourite sacrament,
the time when he gets closest to Olivia,
inhales her perfume, sneezing sometimes

(Bless you, Father,)

and gazes ecclesiastically at her pert nipples
struggling to burst through her pink bra,
distracted briefly by the sun's reflection
through the stained glass window

on to her shiny tights.
Today, she's there again and he glances
at her dark-lined eyes,
wanting to place it on her tongue

but she holds her hand out instead, and he obliges,
– *Corpus Christi*
– *Amen*
and imagines it dropping into her cleavage,

and under the good teaching of Pope Benedict
the XVIth, and the fifteen that went before him,
mere mortals are debarred form searching
the cleavage of young female Communicants

for stray Holy Bread. He indulges his divine
right, and imagines finding it, wedged
in there somewhere. When she turns he watches
her generous bum wiggle,

as her slingback heels tap Morse code
on the mosaic of his existence
hoping his clerical garb hides
his true feelings for her.

Dear Father John Paul,

You have renewed my faith.
You have made me a Christian again,
a Mass-going Roman Catholic
a daily Communicant –
devout,
but it's all a lie, Father John Paul,
it's all a lie.

May God forgive me,
may Pope Benedict XVI forgive me,
may Bishop Peter forgive me.
for I am a hypocrite, Father John Paul.

Every morning at half eight Mass
in St. Valentine's Church,
I'm a hypocrite,
and every day in St. Jude's
National School, I am a hypocrite.
For it is you I truly worship,
you Father, yes you.
It is you I worship.
(Oh dear God forgive me,
for I have broken
the First Commandment.)

It is you I long for. It is to you
I look for salvation,
and I know it's wrong, Father,
I know it's wrong but it's no use,
it is you I worship.

It is for you, in the hope
you might notice me,
that I wear the skirts I wear
and flagellate myself

in these bastards of high heels,
and it is of you I think in the evenings
when I bathe my feet in that awful
concoction of seaweed and Radox,
that my mother has ready.

It is of you I think as I look
at the children in High Infants
picking out the ones I'd like
to have had with you,
and giving them special attention.

It of you I am thinking while Sr. Cuntata
is rambling on about Exodus and Deuteronomy.
It is before you I am kneeling
at the Consecration
and it is your body I am receiving
at Holy Communion,
Father,
Yes, oh yes, it is you.

And when you place it on my hand,
and you do place it on my hand
so gently and so carefully,
it is you, Father John Paul, I am consuming
as I make the sign of the cross
and face the altar,
and turn carefully and slowly
to make the sad journey back
to the fourth row.

What am I to do, Father John Paul?
What am I to do?
I worship your short brown hair.
I worship your bigish nose.
I worship your left ear
which is slightly bigger that your right ear
which I worship too.

And more than anything else,
I worship your mouth and your hands
wishing they were touching me now,
Father John Paul,
and I worship when you sometimes forget
the words of the prayers,
I worship the driver's seat
of your green 1997 Opel Corsa,
and the single bed,
and I am assuming it is a single bed,
that you lie on in the Parochial House
with Father Loula.

I dream of taking ill so you can anoint me.
I dream of being bedridden so you can visit me.
I dream of going to confession
to admit my concupiscence,
so you can hear me.

I dream, Father John Paul,
I dream of someday sending you this letter.
I dream of your reply,
I do, Father John Paul,
I do.

Yours in worship,

Olivia. *xxx*

Single woman, 38, broadminded, gsoh, considered good looking, wanting more from life, breaks it off with bachelor farmer, 56

Oh yes, you were quite a catch alright
with your shiny Massey Ferguson 35X
and the very mention of your new PZ Haybob
was quite simply orgasm inducing,

and in your new Wellingtons, and, perfumed
with silage, you made my eyes water
for the want of you….
But I wasn't enough.

You wanted others too, those slim Friesian
heifers with the shitty tails and dayglo
ear tags, and I was no match for your mother's
washing and cooking and cleaning

or ironing your Greenhills thermal vest
and darning your worn socks with grey wool,
not to mention her masculine prowess
at mucking out the cowhouse.

And so, John James Murphy, I'm breaking up
with you. No more will I wait for you outside
the school hall on Tuesday nights in a skimpy skirt,
hungry eyes penetrating me,

till you finish the seven euro game of twenty-five,
or on Thursday evenings till the mart is over
to be treated in Franco's Formula One Fast Foods,
or make a fool of myself in the yearly Queen

of the Plough Pageant, while you drink porter at the bar
and when it gets warm, and it does get warm,
at the Queen of The Plough Pageant, sweaty even,
and when you remove your jacket

displaying six inches of yellowish longjohns
pulled up over your plaid shirt, will I be there to take
your twenty-year old St. Bernard tweed to the cloakroom,
and look after pink ticket, number 91, for you afterwards.

I'm leaving, John James Murphy, leaving
for Dublin, or England or Mullingar or Navan,
anywhere, away from here, and when I settle
in to my new place, I'll write to you, not to tell you

where I am, and not to say I miss you, but to remind
you that the black cow will be due for calving
on August the twenty-seventh, the day your mother
goes to Knock for the Solemn Novena, and that you had better

find yourself a new girlfriend by then,
or you might have to pull this one yourself.

Days of Fake Tan

I should have refused to get in
once I saw the state
of the inside of the bridal car.
I should have shouted 'no,
I will not marry you,
if this is the way you treat me
on the morning of our special day.'

A hired white Mercedes,
driven by that eejit of a brother
of yours, soon to be my brother-in-law.
Inside, where there should be champagne
and flowers,
a half-bag of calf nuts,
jump leads and a drum of diesel.
I should have ran a mile.
I should have screamed to you
that I would not go through with it.

We could have cancelled
the hotel and the photographer.
Divided the cake.
But I know what you'd have said.
And your mother.
What would it look like
in front of the neighbours
and the expense they had gone to
buying new clothes?
And the talk that'd be in the pub
and around the village for months –
years even.

Your family'd never get over it.
And we couldn't have that.

I bundled up my dress as best I could,
and climbed in to the white Mercedes,
careful not to knock over the half bag
of calf nuts or spill the diesel.

And I told myself that you were a kind
loving and considerate man
who would go to the ends of the earth
for me and your mother
and the neighbours.
That you wouldn't waste money
which was why you had your brother
use our wedding car to feed the calves
in the farm your father bought
when land was cheap.
And that your brother –
my soon to be brother-in-law –
had probably jump started the Hymac
and topped it up with diesel
on his way to collect me.

(I was wrong there.
We diverted round by the Hymac,
and I held the strainer
as he filled the yellow God
with diesel,
and then I climbed into the cab
and turned the starter
as he revved the Mercedes
in an attempt to jump start the digger –
which didn't work.
Together we bled the diesel lines,
him in his hired suit,
me in my white dress and fake tan
without a bridesmaid in sight,
until the airlock was cleared
and the machine purred approval.

Then and only then
did he take me to the church.
Fashionably late,
and stinking of diesel fumes
and calf nuts and dung.)

When you proposed
that we 'sort this thing out,'
I said 'ok,'
because there was no point not to.
I knew that every special occasion
would be choreographed
to accommodate calves and heifers
and cows and bull.
That my birthday,
if you remembered it,
would be moved
to suit the mart schedule
which took priority
and always would take priority.
That our holidays would be an afternoon
in Enniscrone
when the silage was finished.
That our children would be children
of the land.
That I would cook and clean
and milk and drive tractors
and pull calves
and sow and weed and harvest crops.
That getting my hair done
would consist of washing it
with Fairy Liquid
once a week in the back-kitchen sink,
if there was time.

I went through with it
because Johnnie McCormack

married Pauline Finn
last August
and I knew that James Kelly
would never return form America,
and all the girls
I went to the Convent
with were married,
drove their children to school
in Ford Fiestas.
That at thirty-seven,
true romance was for books;
all I'd get was a bid.

I went through with it
because I knew
the days of fake tan
were well and truly behind me.

A Romantic Irishman's Gift to His Wife on Valentine's Day

"I brought you something dear."
"Oh did you? How thoughtful. What is it?"
"A barrow of manure for your azaleas."

Anything to Declare?

"So you're a poet, are you?"
the muscular woman said
in an American accent
as I tried to board a flight
at Shannon
for a holiday at Guantanamo.

I was asked to step aside.
She looked in my eye
for traces of rhyming metre
in my pupils,
for sonnets in my sockets,
for couplets in my cornea.

I was fingerprinted,
footprinted,
dna tested,
testicle weighed,
blood tested,
to see if I was fit.

My poems were x-rayed,
individually examined
the database checked
to see if I was the missing
Arab from Afghanistan,
the Al Qaeda sympathiser
from Killeshandra,
the paedophile from Laois,
the runaway black lesbian
from Tennessee who escaped

the bonfire in 1964,
the County Councillor from Offaly

threatening to resurrect the PDs,
the cat that escaped
from the microwave.

Was I Tailban,
marzipan,
Diazipan,
Madeleine McCann?

Had I outstanding
warrants, subpoenas,
parking tickets,
cloakroom tickets,
did I play cricket?
Fuck, no.
I don't play cricket.

"Guns we can take,
Or bombs in your shoes,
or in the hold,
but suicide–poets,
jihad strategists?"

My cv was checked
my penetration was checked
to see what market share
I had in the poetry industry.

"Are you on the Dow?
What about Q3?
What are your projections
going forward?
Do you have a Power Point
or a website we could look at?
Are your poems any good?"

I was sorry I booked Guantanamo.
It looked nice in the brochure
in the travel agent's.
Cheap too.

I watched the other intending passengers
go through unsearched.
"Why me? Why did you pick on me?"
"You're a poet," she said, "and poets like you
are a threat to the free world."

Date As Postmark

Dear Service User,

You may, or may not, have had a chest x-ray
at Our Lady of Lourdes Hospital, Drogheda,
or at the Midland General Hospital, Portlaoise,
or the Mid Western Regional Hospital, Ennis
(or at any other hospital in Ireland)
we don't know.

And irrespective of the results we gave you at the time,
you may, or may not, have cancer,
we don't know.

If you are experiencing any pain,
or any of the symptoms of this, or any other, disease,
please take something for it – don't ask us what,
we don't know.

Signed:
Minister for Health And Children,
on behalf of
The Health Service Executive,
The Government, and
the People of Ireland.

Misé Eire 2009

After Pádraic Pearse, George Morrison, Sean Ó Riada, Eavan Boland and Kevin Higgins.)

The repo man lifted the jeep today.
Pity, that.
It was useful to live in since we lost the house.

Testing

I watched the man
with the dodgy hip
offer his car
to the soul searching
of the Castlerea
NCT centre,
and I wondered
would the testing pass
and would the man's
hip get better or worse,
in sickness
and in Health Centres,
where the likes of him waited
for a form
to give to the girl
with no English,
and him with no Irish,
at a hospital reception
in five years time,
for a replacement hip.

The men in the white suits,
with clipboards and computers,
and ramps and revving,
and smoke tests and rust tests
and brake tests,
test the car
for roadworthiness,
and I wondered
if we'd get the chance
to test the roads
for car-worthiness
some day,
and reject them
as our cars were rejected
today.

I thought him lucky,
the man with the dodgy hip,
at least
he could take the train,
unless
he was from Gortaganny
or Glenamaddy,
or going
to Tuam
or Tarmonbarry
unless
it was Tuesday
when he could take the bus.
Was it Tuesday?
No.
Wednesday.
Where would he wait
for the Six Days?
Tully's Hotel maybe,
or has that been turned
into luxury apartments?

I watched a man once
with an ass and cart –
drunk he was too,
the man,
not the ass,
and his cart
passed everything
and he got home safely,
and I wondered
where he was now.

House to Yourself

It's great to get the house to yourself for a while.
You can do things you wouldn't get away with
in front of herself.
Things you wouldn't do in public,
like clipping your toenails in the kitchen
where the light is better.

Hooded crows

explode from the sycamores.
A lonesome collie announces
neighbours, or maybe distant relatives
arriving for the removal.

"Poor old John Joe,
he was a decent skin."
"Never a bad word for anyone,"
heads gently nodding agreement.

Kathleen offers currant cake
and strong tea in striped mugs –
the bride that might have been
had she not stayed to look after her mother.

It won't be long now
till time reclaims this house,
and the hooded crows fly through
on their way back to the sycamores.

(This poem is dedicated to the late M Kelly Lombardi,
teacher, sage, poet, friend, who loved Italy her spiritual
home and Mayo, Ireland, her ancestral home.)

Ritual

In our best clothes
and marinated in Brut,
we headed out the door
at eight or maybe half past,
thumbing
and knowing
there were no cars on the road –
a pessimistic optimism;
a triumph of hope over history.
And the cars that never came
didn't bring us,
but somehow we got there –
because we wanted.

A few fast pints
if we were served,
then onward
to the Sunday night dance
in the Town Hall.
Bouncers greeted
in maroon jackets
and ridiculous dickey-bows.
We heard the band warming-up
as we counted our change:
"Testing, one, two,
testing, one two."

Businesslike, we headed left
like in Church
to the men's side,
for it was business –
we were hoping for a return
on our investment.
The architect,

obviously not a dancer,
put the toilets
the other way round,
maybe he was just
taking the piss,
or the builder
held the plans upside down.

When the testing was done
they started:
"A few fast numbers,
ladies and gentlemen,"
and the stampede
across the waxed maple
for the hand,
or more likely
the sulk,
of the girl of our dreams.
always, it seemed,
the object of the dreams
of all the men, lads and boys, there.

And they all reached for her,
vultures picking at the flesh;
sometimes we were worried
her arms would be disconnected
under that tight red jumper,
counting ourselves lucky
to get a quick scent of her Charlie
as she passed us
on her way to the floor.

We wouldn't pull, of course,
so we headed for the men's toilets,
glad they were on the women's side,
trying to make it look
like that's where we were headed

all along,
not wanting to confess
the mortal sin of rejection.
Maybe the architect
was himself a sinner,
and knew we'd need sanctuary
someday,
from ourselves.

And then somewhere
it happened,
inexplicably and inevitably,
the vocabulary of the night
punctuated by flailing arms
and weighty punches.
"Who do you think you're pushing?"
"Hold my jacket."
"I'll see you outside."

The maroon-clad mercenaries
involved themselves
and in the pulling and dragging
sweating and swearing,
we noticed the girl
in the red jumper
disappear
under the arm
of a scrawny townie,
and with them,
our hopes
for the week.

Outside the losers took stock –
swore revenge,
torn suits and blood stained shirts –
you could easily mistake them
for the winners.

We were glad to take the lift
in the Mini or Cortina,
that last hundred yards,
after walking six miles,
stopping at roadside wells
trying to satisfy

our thirst for life.

Paddy Naughton

                        lay in bed
the morning of his sixty-sixth birthday.
On the locker, a mug with his teeth,
a battery clock and the gold watch
from his colleagues after forty three years
as a postman.

He won't miss the run, he tells himself.
It had changed.
Gone was the welcome of Campbells,
glazed with plywood
by some relative in England
when Nora was put into the mental home,
and the hippies that moved in
to where old Pete Reilly had lived,
or the Dublin crowd in Shaughnesseys.
Not the same, any of them.
Nor the three generations of Kirbys,
he could never remember whose wife was who,
and as for the children,
where did they get the strange names for them?

He wouldn't miss the dogs, the cats,
the stench from Mrs. Hession's clothes
as she leant on the bonnet of the van
to tell him nothing.
Or O'Connors,
and trying to get the solicitor's letters signed
when Donal went off
with the skinny remedial teacher,
leaving poor Denise to sort out the mess.
He wouldn't miss the hens outside Flynn's,
(and inside too, he suspected,)
or the complaints of the Widow Hunt,

when he didn't call before three.
"How can I deal with my business
at this hour of the day?"
Or the parcels for Kennedy one
who ran some sort of a mail-order business
over the internet,
or the ESB bills, Eircom bills
and bags of election literature
and promotions from DIY Stores
and the postcards offering paint jobs
promising to last a lifetime,
for the hundred and ninety-three houses he served.

He wouldn't miss the potholes,
or the tractors with slurry tankers
or round bales,
blocking the road.
He wouldn't miss the cold mornings
or the constant rain
or the branches whipping the windscreen
on borheens leading to pensioners
who rarely went out.

He'd miss none of it.
Not even the twenty-pound notes
and glasses of whiskey at Christmas
from the old stock,
which led to the broken mirrors and dents on the van.
And he wondered what time his replacement,
Pake Ronan's son,
would call today, and what he'd bring.
Would it be a birthday card
from his sister in Chicago who never forgot,
or a letter from the Health Board
calling him for a check-up?

He sat up, looked at the clock,
he was at Dixon's at this time yesterday,
and the day before,
and every working day
since the vans replaced the bicycles.

He leant forward and picked up the watch,
blew onto the glass and wiped it with his sleeve,
the last thing he needed really – time.
He leant again, this time reaching
for his Digoxin tablets,
tipping them on to the duvet
before counting out the days they'd last.

Abandoned Railway

They've cleared the overgrowth
from the railway, closed
in nineteen-seventy-five,
after eighty years.
They've repaired the fences –
replaced the mileposts.
Removed the barbed wire
crossing the track,
erected by farmers whose cattle
had grazed undisturbed
on bright spring afternoons.

Horsetail and thistles fold under my feet.
I walk these sleepers
between Kiltimagh and Claremorris –
through our farm by the lake,
and I think of my ancestors
on a one-way ticket.

I see simply crafted steel gates,
riveted and rusted, rotted timbers,
reminders of hard-drawn copper wire,
on once proud telegraph poles
that carried signals
to gatekeepers at level-crossings
– the one-fifty-five
or the three-ten
often running late.

I see the faces of children
pressed against the window,
counting the fields
on school tours,
and the suitcases of tourists
on the annual outing
to Salthill.

I glance at sheds and backs of houses
gardens with onions and cabbage
and potato stalks beginning to flower.
I look down again quickly,
to check my steps
on the rotted oak, careful
not to miss the inconsistent spacing
at the joint in the metals.

This was the railway my uncle worked on,
checking the sleepers and wedges –
the bolts and the joints,
the fences and the signals.

This was the track the train ran on –
the train that took his brother and his sister.
his cousins and his neighbours
to Cobh,
to board a ship to America.

This was the railway that brought
the youth from Sligo;
from Collooney and from Leyny;
from Tubercurry, Curry and Charlestown;
from Swinford, Kiltimagh and Claremorris;
from Ballindine, Milltown and Castlegrove;
from Tuam, Ballyglunin and Athenry,
where immigrants joined
from Galway and Woodlawn,
Ballinasloe and Athlone.

This track collected them
from Croughwell and Loughrea;
from Ardrahan, Gort and Tubber;
from Crusheen and Ennis
where the West Clare Railway
evacuated hopefuls
and surrendered them to emigration.

This track carried the train
from Ardsollus and Quin;
from Ballycar & Newmarket;
from Sixemilebridge and Cratloe;
from Meelick and Longpavement into Limerick
on to Kilonan and Boher,
to Dromkeen and Pallas,
from Oola and Limerick Junction
where he
and they
changed trains
going to Emly,
Knocklong and Kilmallock,
Charleville, Buttevant and Mallow,
Mourne Abbey, Rathduff, Blarney and Cork,
through Tivoli, Dunkettle and Littleisland,
Glounthaune, Fota and Carrigaloe,
through Rushbrooke and on to Cobh,

never to return.

Never Black

"What colour is the sky today?" you asked.
I wanted to say it was blue.
"Grey," I said.

"Dark grey or light grey?"
"Both," I said.
You said: "I'm really lucky,
the sky is always blue –
azure during the day,
indigo in the evening
and Prussian blue at night,
but never black.
It's never black."

The flowers are always in bloom
where you are Mother,
intense,
the grasses a fertile green
never need mowing.
The weeds behave themselves
like you wished I'd had
when I was six and seven.

Now you are six and seven,
and getting even younger.
Getting even.
                Younger.

Your Field

I watched you steer the plough
drawn by a faithful bay mare,
cultivating an existence
on unforgiving Mayo hills.

Together you turned the sod,
under the scrutiny of birds,
circling, before they swooped
to pluck the fresh food.

We planted you late that summer
harvested before your time.
Barley and hay awaiting collection,
gathered with heavy hearts.

Now I watch a younger man
steer a shiny green tractor
skilfully around shrubs,
flower beds and a garden swing.

His young son watches every move,
as he stands beside his mother,
in the comfort of the bungalow
built on your field.

Posts and Wire

                    divide the land,
keep sheep from grazing
and solicitors busy
where the wire doesn't work.

Brothers with borders.

Yet we all came with nothing
and will leave the same way,
coffins unable to accommodate
the vast tracts of land
acquired at auctions.
Their turn will come round –
underbidders will say farewell
beside the final acquisition.
The grass will grow
on both sides of the fence
                    regardless.

They Cut-down the Trees

Oaks, sycamore,
a row of ash
planted by my grandfather
in 1931,
and green gorse
sprinkled with seasonal yellow,
all swept away
by a 65-tonne Komatsu dozer
guided by Swavic Jaworski –
on the Friday afternoon
of the June holiday weekend.

They built an industrial park,
with its signwritten vans,
articulated lorries
and factories –
grey clad with blue trim,
yielding components
for American companies
with tax-free concessions,
or surgical gadgets
for comatose patients,
or components or cabling
for automotive or aeronautical
instrumentation,
or kitchens direct
from factory to mortgage,
or sheeting
for shrink wrapping,
or tracking devices
for missiles,
or moulds for casting
garden gnomes
or terracotta flower pots.

Drivers of forklifts
load stillages,
and Dexion racking,
conveyors,
and union-free robots,
oily and busy,
and nibblers and rollers,
and three-phase compressors,
with motors and filters,
labour on,
where I used to play football
with bigger boys,
in spring evenings
and weekends.

They built a ring-road
with an entrance
at the town goal,
encircling car parks
with grey Toyotas,
Silver Mondeos,
red Astras –
waiting obediently
on finance;
their busy owners,
thinking of their offspring
in crèches or summer-camp,
and longing for their cheap
packaged fortnight in the sun.

I look at the board,
where I imagined the stand,
where crowds roared
as the young boy
out-performed his elders
and lifted the cup;
I read the business names

and the twenty-word
descriptions and I hope.

I sincerely hope
that a tree-nursery
might take up the lease
on the vacant,
Unit 77.

Mick Donlon

       sits on the bank
and listens to the smooth swish
of the Garcia reel as he casts–out,
using live worms for bait,
clearing bulrushes; watching
the splash as the lead–weight sinks
the meaty hook and pulls
against the red polystyrene float.

When the ripples disappear,
Mick stares, first towards the water,
then the hills – neighbour's houses
– McLoughlin's, Connolly's
and the other Donlon's –
no relation.

Then downwards again
to the fresh water of Culintra lake
and swears he can see
the scowl of his nagging wife,
of thirty-five years.

He wonders how and why her image
follows him even to this,
the only spot in the week,
where he takes time for himself.

He reels in, more to dissipate
the reflection, than in hope
of catching a perch,
and wonders,
if she'll nag him forever
when they're both in the grave.

The Waking

He says it's the waking that gets him.
Waking next to where she used to lie
and wishing she was there
or he was not.

Neighbours gathered for the wake,
smoked pipes, told stories and drank,
when the cheap whiskey was gone
he produced the pure drop –
hand made in the valley.

The dew obscures his vision of her.
He wakes screaming.
He can't remember her face
after forty-one years.

He says it's the waking that gets him.

A Life

You spent years going to dances.
The Maple, The Arcadia
and festival marquees
pitched in after-grass
and if the one you liked wouldn't shift
you pretended you liked
the one you shifted.

You shifted Noreen Cassidy in 1968
but her father shifted you
when he heard about you after Mass.
You had an eye for Anne Danaher
and for her cousin from Manchester
in the yellow hot-pants.
You couldn't understand
when Kathleen Byrne
refused you in 1972.
Her land was next to yours.

You drank bottles of stout
with three generations of lads
and made smart comments
about their girlfriends
behind their back.
You were waiting, you said,
for a good-looking young one –
someone with prospects.
Someone like Teresa Dowd –
the District Nurse.

She found you last Friday –
stretched in the cottage for over a week.
Fourteen thousand stuffed
behind a plate in the dresser:
a picture of Big Tom on the mantelpiece.

Lovers

He had long hair.
She, a short temper.

He, his Dad's Toyota.
She, her mother's Rothmans.

He, her name tattooed.
She had his child.

He never sent money.
She never finished school.

Going Through Your Things

We found them in the strangest places –
blue twenty-pound notes –
in cups on the dresser,
in westerns with big print,
and a bundle in the freezer.
Fifty-two of them; stashed carefully
just in case we needed anything.

Ireland – October 4th, 2005

Today on the news they were on about money again.
Money wasted on a computer for the Health Service.
A hundred and fifty million they said.
Some expert said it was a hundred and seventy.
Million.
Money wasted.
It's not wasted they said, we have the computers.
So it's not wasted.
It's not wasted.
We have the computers.

Today on the news they were on about money again.
Sometimes they can't get through.
Can't get an answer on the phone.
The women.
On the helpline – they can't get an answer.
There isn't enough staff to answer the phone.
So they'll have to wait.
Wait for another while.
Wait for an answer, wait for help.
Wait in the fear and the violence.
Wait for an answer.

We have the computers but no one to answer.

Removal

In a trendy Georgian doorway
on a sunny April morning,
Milo lies dreaming
of a time before he lost his place
in the order of things.

In the next doorway,
Kate too sleeps soundly.
He never carried her
across a threshold.
Neither ever had one,
wouldn't be admitted anyway
anywhere on the Southside.

Soon the tourists will come.
Sultry Mediterranean girls
in short skirts,
heels clicking time
with their conversation.
Long dark hair swinging
as they analyse the sights.
And Americans with shirts
as loud as their criticism of Bush,
the weak Dollar and
how affluent Dublin has become.

Suddenly a vehicle pulls up.
Milo, startled, looks.
They grab him –
before he can react he's in the back.
They go for Kate –
and soon Annie,
Jimmo and Thomas are in
and the van is pulling away.

Swiftly across the Liffey –
in a few minutes
they're on the street again.
Out of sight of the sultry Mediterranean girls
with the short skirts and clicking heels.
Even the Americans.

Milo knows it's no use going back.
Not till October.
The tourists will be gone then.

Ireland's special branch –
the anti-litter squad
are back in Store Street,
enjoying coffee and gateau
after washing their hands and
evicting the homeless.

A Different Way of Life

Half seven, but if you're tired
it might be quarter to eight,
you'll dash to the hayshed
and take the hay-knife
from where you left it last night.

Before you'll have chance
to slice the hay with all your might
they will be lowing – hearing you,
and you'll shout something at them
about patience and gratitude.

You'll carry it on a fork
to the cowhouse,
to three hungry cows
whose sideways glance says
'hurry on with that we're starving.'

You always feed the blue cow first –
she is the leader,
followed as she is in from the fields
every evening by the black one,
then the white one
who isn't really white –
she has a dash of white on her head –
sufficient to distinguish her
form the one that's completely black.

They'll munch contentedly while you
get the three legged stool
and the two gallon galvanised bucket
and milk them in the same order.

Sometimes the cat will sit at the door
to remind you of his existence.
You might aim a single squirt at him –

and get him in the eye,
but the face is generally accepted
as a hit.
You'll smile – he'll run.

The whistling of the milk into
the empty bucket
then the changing sound
as it fills and you can tell
how much is in without looking,

The careful pouring
through the strainer
into the churns keeping
half a sweetcan for the house.

Then you'll release the cows
to the freedom of brown pastures
and with the grape, and then the spade
and the brush,
you'll clean away the manure
and last night's bedding
and replace it –
fresh for the evening.

Then you'll go into the house,
wash and change
into your school clothes
and sit with your mother
who'll have three rashers fried,
a couple of sausages
and maybe an egg,
and it'll be your turn to munch,
maybe on the way to catch the bus
at half past

and study for seven hours –
a different way of life.

Vision

When the sun burns off the fog
and full visibility returns,
I wonder if I'll be able to see
the mistakes I made yesterday?

Nothing

A red float waltzes on the welcoming water of Caher lake,
a light breeze deceives in the August afternoon sun.
Seamus checks his new hat from the end of the boat –
a birthday gift from his sister Kate in Sheffield,
as he accepts another Sunday ritual
when even the fish are on holiday.

Yellow silage fields watch the calm water from a discrete distance.
In other fields, white and yellow bungalows are planted randomly.
Sitka spruce matures in the wetlands near water's edge,
Somewhere, a fund manager factors-in the European grant.
A sudden click of the grey reel and Seamus is upright,
staring motionless, before he starts to wind.

Nothing.

Seamus re-casts, careful not to dislodge the hat –
at least a size too small,
and sits again and dreams of the night he left his hand
on Ann Buckley's knee at Joe Dolan –
funny, he thought, neither married after.

The still silence is broken by the roar
of a blue Yamaha jetski approaching from the east –
the pilot no more than twenty,
short black hair and a green "No Fear" tee-shirt.
Petrol fumes, exhaust and a tidal parting in its wake.

"Wanker."

Seamus covers his bald patch with a dirty hankie and swears
that next week he'll bring the shotgun for when the jetski returns
to tease the boat and scare the fish that aren't there.
He draws the line in slowly as if a twenty-pounder were on the end,
and puts away the rod as silence creeps back to the lake.

Autumn 1944

(After Richard Koenig)

A greyscale woman,
in a check coat
with patches on the back,
wearing clogs
that are too big –
battered by time
and the time
in which she lives,
stares at a list
on a Parisian door –
reading the names
of the newly dead,
hoping her son
is not on the page,
remembering
kissing
him goodbye,
on the platform
at Gare du Nord,
only six weeks previously
and agreeing with him
that everything
would be ok,
the war would end
soon, and they'd
be reunited
with his father,
who made
the same journey
four years previously
and wrote at first.
Then the letters

stopped,
and so did her heart
for a while.
Today
she wonders,
where her son
is and if she'll ever
listen to jazz
as she strolls through
Montmartre
on Sunday afternoons,
with them both
again.

By the Fire

There where his youth used to stand
is a man nearly fifty just back from a music lesson,
who falls asleep by the fire in the evening like the old people.
Maybe some of them mastered the guitar
but mostly they died, empty.

A boy in short trousers can't understand what all the fuss is about
as visiting neighbours lament the death of a man from the town.
He was only forty they said. Only forty.
Only forty?
Did he expect to live forever?

For a while the man of nearly fifty is young again.
His supple fingers arch the neck of the Strat
and press and pluck strings to an audience
of men and women in the town – some surviving forty.

May you build a ladder to the stars
And climb on every rung…
He awakes and pokes at the embers realising
George got it wrong.
As he places another sod he says to no-one
"Youth is vested in the young."

Object of Desire

In a secondary school uniform –
jumper as grey as clouds
on a rainy Connemara day
and a skirt that she's growing out of,
on temporary release
for a lunch break
where cigarettes are the special of the day
and the talk is of boys and men and the like.

I notice her.

Today she has a few more freckles
on her arms and on her face
and on her heart.
We exchange silent smiles and go
about our business as if
nothing has happened.

I imagine asking her to marry me
and later watch as she swims naked
to the church, to whisper 'I do',
turning into a shout for all to hear –
loud as a blast from the horn of a ship
on a foggy night.

Dad

        was the weekend once a month
when you watched your mother scrub
the bathroom before he came, and herself,
in it, after he left,

        was the one who gave you the gold
chain to keep you quiet after he found you,
under your nightdress on the October Bank
holiday weekend, 1994,

        and the bright red coat you wanted,
a year later, when he forced you to perform
in his respectable navy Volvo
on the way home from the pictures,
(*Bad Company* you think it was, starring
Ellen Barkin,)

        and the beating he said was a game
as he pleasured in the back bedroom
while your mother had her hair done
for the Christmas party, the next day.

Dad was the banker who was promoted
to Area, and later General, Manager, the man
tipped for a directorship, till his body
was found with eight separate gunshot wounds

        on New Year's Eve, 2008.

Shrine

In a field in November rain,
a butcher in a blood-stained coat
chops liver –
his cleaver rising and falling
to the beat of disco music,
keeping his head down,
chopping.
And the strippers come
and wiggle bits
to the music,
throwing their skimpy clothes
on whitethorns,
careful to avoid the mud
in silver heels,
careful.
And middle-aged men
with mobile phones
and dirty raincoats,
watch from the bushes,
panting and drooling,
imagining.
A fire burns in the corner
to keep the naked women warm;
a small man pitchforks
lambs, and other fuel
to keep it burning.
Other women, older,
recite the rosary,
solemnly,
and prayers for lost souls.

Kidney and Clutch Kebabs

Preheat the kitchen to 180 degrees.
Remove all loose clothing,
dismantle the lever and rod,
skin, core and halve the kidneys
making sure the lever base
is correctly located in the housing pivot.
Cut the rashers of bacon in half and roll up
and secure in position with the retaining clips.
Thread the ingredients alternatively
on to eight skewers,
lubricate all pivot points
and bearing surfaces with silicone grease –
reassemble in the following order:
kidney, tomato, tensioner, bacon,
pressure-plate, onion; then repeat
and manoeuvre the assembly into position
finishing with bacon.
Brush with melted butter and refit
the housing retaining bolts and tighten
them to the specified torque setting.

Serve on a bed of rice.

And Another Thing

                            don't
forget to put the cat down
before you come to bed,
and no farting while my head
is under the duvet.

And another thing,
leave the motorbike in the hall,
don't try bringing it upstairs again,
the smell of petrol
gives me a headache
and you know what happens
when I get a headache.

And another thing,
I don't know if it was the Vaseline
you put on the Swiss roll
or the meths that gave me heartburn
and don't try telling me
it was the splash of paraffin I added –
you must admit, it does look
like red lemonade.

And another thing,
you disgust me.
You come home every night, drunk,
expecting a ride and a side salad,
and maybe a game of darts
when we've finished.

Have you put that cat down yet?

And On Sundays

you read the TV guide in the papers –
but you don't have a TV,
dinners are mostly warmed-up takeaways
from first-floor Orientals,
and in the evening you sip cheap
Western Cape (or is it Tesco?) screw-top white,
and later listen through the paper party walls,
to the soundtrack of the lovemaking
of the young couple next door but one
of these days you will write
into your leather-bound vellum A4 desk diary,
an entry into the unknown world
and risk your no-claims bonus
with Angela form Accounts Payable
with the maroon Focus who takes three
weeks holidays with her cats
every year in Monte Carlo.

On Mondays

you do what you do every other day of the week –
dream through the glass partition, of opening
the top button of her blouse, and the second and the third
time you answer that damn phone which keeps ringing
in your head until you tell the caller to fuck off,
there's no support for Windows Vista yet, and why
didn't they stick with XP which was working fine?
And at lunchtime, and you know you shouldn't, you kick
the aluminium foil tray the Romaniac gypsy woman
uses for begging and feel sorry after,
as the scurrying coins, all two euro and seventeen cent,
drop through the gulley into the sewer of your existence,
but you can't stoop to reinstate her dignity and your own
so you head to the pub and blur the image of Angela
as best you can, wondering, as you do, what colour
her bra is.

18

In Centra on Thursday –
the day his dole money came through,
Paddy queued behind the Poles
and Latvians in high-vis jackets,

and the woman from Nigeria
with the four children,
and he wondered where Nigeria
was and where Ireland had gone.

Maria was from Saskatchewan,
he was glad he didn't have to write it.
"Canada," she explained,
"just the corned beef and firelighters?"

Later, in O'Shaughnessey's,
the Surinamese barman
rushed him a pint of Guinness,
his change and a receipt.

"Where the fuck's that?"
"Northern South America, sir."
At 23.10, a Garda in a turban
politely asked him to leave the premises.

In the Chinese, he ordered Number 18 –
unable to pronounce Szechwan,
but knowing he liked the spices.
The girl behind the counter

was from the Philippines – he asked
her what part of China that was.
In his fourth-floor flat, Paddy lit a fire
and settled to watch satellite porn

starring a German blonde
and a brunette from Ballyvary –
he thought he knew her uncle.
Later he drank Red Bull and jumped

out the window to his death
proving that you can't fly
after drinking Red Bull,
unless you could before.

In Farmers Fields

(With sincerest apologies to the late John McCrae)

In farmers' fields the rushes grow
between the buachallan, row on row
that mark our place; and in the sky
bits of silage covers fly –
left over after the winter.

We're in REPS. Ten days ago
the inspector called; his face aglow
giving out he was
about the state of farmers' fields.

Take up our quarrel with the foe:
he'll cut our payment; that we know.
This place be yours don't let them get too high
If we lose the payment we'll surely die.
A famine; though rushes grow
In farmers' fields.

Election Manifesto

It is after long and solemn consideration
that I have decided to place my name
before you, to offer myself
as a candidate in the forthcoming election,

to throw my hat into the ring.
It was not an easy decision.
I come from a long line
of non-candidates. There were hopes

from an early age that our family
would be a proud political dynasty –
generation after generation –
of people that didn't bother.

Non-principled, non-acting,
non-candidates.
But there comes a time in the life of a man
when he has to take a stand,

when he can no longer ignore
what is happening,
when he can't remain passive.
That time has come for me

which is why I am asking you today
to consider very carefully
your position on polling day.
Do not cast your mark lightly –

remember those who do not have your opportunity –
the oppressed,
the disenfranchised,
victims of cruel dictatorships,

and remember that it does not matter
who you vote for –
your vote does not count,
democracy is a state of mind –

an illusion, a delusion,
a joke played on you,
so consider my candidacy carefully.
I have no policies.

I have no wish to make this a better country.
I am not for or against anything.
I only want the salary,
expenses and pension for myself.

Please remember me when you cast your vote.
A vote for me is a vote for you,
the endorsement of your right to be ignored,
overlooked, forgotten.

Together let us celebrate democracy.
Remember me on polling day.

Visitors

Knock.
Go.
"Hello."
Sit.
Tea.
Biscuits.
Cake.
Talk.
Hope.
Go.
No.

The Journey

Creaking hinges signalled her arrival
the organist confirmed in tune,
curiosity got heads turning
ceremonies would be underway soon.

Mammies in hats and smiling dentures
nodded approval as she crept by,
bachelors in pinstripes regretted
some of them even wanted to cry.

Her father stepped proudly beside her
quantifying the cost of the meals,
neighbours with disposables snapped them
while bridesmaids struggled in heels.

Travelling from faraway places
relatives not seen for a while,
fashions from Paris and Dunne's
perfume that would kill from a mile.

But nightmares haunted her journey
first love and smouldering old flames,
nights of amorous encounters
memories weren't all that remained.

In-laws stood waiting to be appointed
fresh roses decorated the pew,
she advanced to the altar divided
between destiny and the true love she knew.

Rhythmic footsteps took her nearer
heartbeats discounted the day,
the kaleidoscope of colour distracted
a voracious urge to run away.

Decision-time boldly confronted
but her heart ducked hopelessly aside,
as the groom stepped forward unaware
of the thoughts tormenting his bride.

Numbly going through the motions
trembling on the cold altar floor,
she reflected on past misadventures
until she couldn't tolerate anymore.

Suddenly alive again and turning
to shocked faces she did declare,
her love for the one not present
to the amazement of everyone there.

An Open Letter to the Purchasing Department of Mid West Farmers Co-Operative Society; All other Farmers Co-Operative Societies Please Copy

Dear Sir or Madam,

Being a frequent customer of your store,
I have noticed the downturn in sales recently,
and to return your turnover to its former levels,
I humbly make the following suggestion.

My gender identity
(and there are many like me)
is such that I often need
to express myself in a feminine fashion.

As a direct consequence of this,
I need to purchase both male and female clothing.
I have found that none of the women's clothes
in Dunne's Stores fit me,

and that the staff there are indifferent, to put it mildly,
to men of my age seeking to try on skirts, blouses,
dresses, and other, smaller items,
especially in the ladies changing rooms.

(Now I must point out that there is no signage
whatsoever which expresses clearly
that the changing rooms are for women-only in Dunne's,
or that people like myself are debarred

from using these changing rooms.
I have had many embarrassing moments
in these situations, and don't want to put myself
in such a position again.)

Anyway, what I suggest is that your co-operative
offer a range of ankle, knee and thigh-high boots
with six-inch heels in a range of sizes
from nine to say, fifteen.

(The McLoughlin Brothers have very big feet.)
I must stress that these boots
will not need steel toe-caps,
nor are they to be confused with the excellent range

of wellingtons your store carries.
And the heels will need to be of the stiletto type.
I know that you will be confused and concerned
that these thin heels might easily become lodged in cattle slats

or puncture silage covers,
but I assure you that this type of footwear
is not intended for use in such locations.
Having personally had much difficulty

in adapting inner tubes of the large tractor wheels
for use as skirts,
(I had a lot of difficulty with the valve especially,)
may I suggest that you contact Dunlop

or Bridgestone and ask them to supply a range
of properly made rubber skirts
in waist sizes from thirty-six
possibly up as far as seventy-two

for the bigger dairy farmers.
One of the challenges facing our community
is the difficulty we have copying exactly,
the female shape.

Could I suggest that you would perhaps contact
your various suppliers,
and seek their assistance
in producing products

which you could market as the Dolly Range –
and lest there be any confusion,
our community wants to look
like the female country singer

and not the cloned sheep.
(That said, if you do have any contact details
for the sheep-coning lab in the UK,
don't lose their number

in case it would be needed
after you take in the supplies I suggest.)
I write in desperation.
I have sought supplies elsewhere

in this area without success.
I rang Beatrice O'Donnell
of Beatrice's Bridal Boutique
in Barnadearg

about getting a larger range of bridal wear,
but she was somehow confused
and said that if I was looking for halters,
the best place to look was the Ballinasloe Horse Fair.

And Geraldine Farragher
in Farraher's Fashions in Ahascaragh
said something about having to ring the Gardai
when I enquired if her suppliers offered

convent uniforms in larger sizes.
She said she'd get back to me but hasn't as yet.
To back-up my request,
the organisation I represent has

commissioned independently
verifiable figures to demonstrate our needs.
Ninety six percent of our members
are either bachelors or separated.

Ninety three percent wear their mother's clothes;
and of these eight-seven percent
of the mothers have been dead for twenty years or more,
and as you can imagine

this is not a very satisfactory situation.
(Most of the clothes are showing signs of wear
and are well out of fashion.)
A staggering one hundred and fourteen percent

buy the Farmer's Journal every week
to see if any suitable clothing
is available in the classifieds.
Our organisation has been in touch

with the Irish Farmers Association
who said it was best
to deal with this matter at local level.
I appeal to you to consider the request

of my organisation.
I believe that it will increase your turnover
and shareholder value
and bring much satisfaction, pleasure and joy

to our members
in these tough times for farmers.

Mise le meas,
Pól McAnEaspag, (also know as Pólin)
Runai, East Galway Crosdressers Guild
Affiliated to Crossdressers Ireland.

Disgusting

You won't believe it Maura.
He came at me last night
with a yoke you could hang
a pot of spuds on.
It must be the steak
I gave him for his tea.
Seven ninety-five it was,
in SuperValu.
I don't go to Lidl.
You don't know where
they get it from.

And he meant it.
Wanted to get at me, he did.
Well I'll tell you Maura,
I was having none of it.
I told him he hadn't mentioned it sooner.
I wasn't ready.
I'll get chicken for tonight.
Safer.

I suppose he'll be like that
for the week.
He goes that way.
After me every night
'till it goes off him.
Disgusting.

I should have known.
The blonde young one
was on the telly
on about foreign holidays.
Legs and tits everywhere.
But I think the steak
had something to do with it.
For seven ninety-five
you'd want to be getting
a bit of peace.

Like something
out of the circus he was.
Parading it round the room
in front of him.
Showing it off to me.
Letting me know
it was still working.
Putting me on notice.

Chicken is safer.
I'll get a chicken for tonight.
I'll check the RTE Guide.
Make sure it's safe
for him to watch.
Safe for me, I mean.
There's nothing more disgusting
than that sort of thing
when you're not expecting it.
Not ready for it Maura,
do you know what I mean?

At his age.
Pure disgusting.
You'd think it would
have gone off him by now.

Then he asked me
to handle him.
Filthy.
The very thought of it
is putting me off the chicken already.

Absolutely revolting.
Nearly as bad as the time
he asked me to…
No. No, I won't say it.
I can't let it pass my lips.

Oh To Own My Own Chip Shop

I'd sell chips in all shapes and sizes;
thin ones, fat ones,
white frozen ones,
brown home-cut ones,
fried in oil –
and I'd have a range of oils –
from heavy industrial Ducham's
to extra light, extra virgin
sun-kissed sunflower olive oil.
I'd even offer a range of chips
shallow fried in Vaseline,
and menthol flavoured fries,
lightly coated with Vicks.
I'd offer burgers for all tastes,
different shapes and textures,
Hawaiian, curried, regular,
quarter-pounders, half pounders,
even the full pounder.
Yes the full pounder.
Single burgers, double burgers,
triple burgers and my own favourite,
the quadruple – named after the bypass.
My burgers would have everything:
cheese, grated or sliced,
fresh or mouldy,
Edam, Cheddar, Mozzarella,
and with onions, jalapenos, chillies,
mayonnaise, coleslaw, more onions –
all embraced by a floury soft bun
baked by the rounded Mrs Sweeney,
and her daughter Kathleen,
in the back kitchen of their cottage
near Swinford.
I'd offer kebabs,

with the sweat dripping off them,
and curries that would have you running for days –
you'd be ready for the marathon
after my curries,
and onion rings, and tomato rings –
even a range of wedding rings
for starry eyed couples
who called before going to a nightclub.
(I'd even do a range of rings for same sex unions
but that's a different matter altogether.)
And pizzas. Did I mention pizzas?
Four-inch and six inch
and eight inch and ten inch
and twelve inch
that would take you ages to get your mouth around
and eighteen inch for the tractor drivers in season –
the silage season,
and southern fried chicken,
and Western Brand chicken,
and deep fried chicken,
and my special for the bachelors in their forties
and frustrated businessmen –
the pullet of the day.
In the back,
but I'd bring her out sometimes,
I'd have a busty Lithuanian,
battering sausages and a range of fish –
fresh and frozen.
And cooked too of course.

Why do I want my own chipshop, you ask?
My father had a chipshop in Ballindine.
He fell fowl of the Western Health Board,
the Cash and Carry
and the seven bookies in the town.
His father had a chip shop in Crumlin
after moving from Frosinone in 1964.
It's run by my cousin now.

My uncle has a chipshop in Lanesborough.
My other uncle has a chipshop
in New Twopothouse,
not to be confused with Old Twopothouse.
(My aunt shamed the family.
I can't mention her name
in front of my poor mother.
She did the unmentionable;
the despicable.
She married...
She married into a Chinese in Swanlinbar.)

It's what we do us Buonarrotis,
we run chipshops.
It's what we are.
It's the gel that holds our hair in place;
the pigment that colours our skin,
our oxygen.
And one day soon, I'll have my own,
I have checked out a place in Bohola,
The rent is low and it's on the N5.
Buonarroti's of Bohola,
I like the taste of it already.

Half-Eleven Mass

And the priest breathed in,
And the congregation breathed in,
And the priest opened his mouth to deliver the word of God,
And the congregation opened their ears to receive the word of God,
And the priest began to deliver the word of God,
And it went over the heads of the congregation,
And out the door and down the street,
To Aldi, where the thoughts of the congregation were queuing,
For the hairdryers for two–ninety-nine at twelve o'clock.
And the priest was glad that he was bald,
And the congregation was glad that he was bald,
And Aldi were sad that he was bald.
One less hairdryer at two–ninety-nine
At twelve o'clock.

About the Author

John Corless lives and writes in County Mayo, Ireland. His poetry is a mix of political, satirical and rural and has been described as 'Paul Durcan meets The Sawdoctors.' He has an MA in Creative Writing from Lancaster University (2008) and is currently researching for a PhD. He writes poetry, fiction and drama. His work has been published in magazines and collections worldwide. He teaches creative writing in the Castlebar campus of GMIT (Galway Mayo Institute of Technology). This is his first collection.